Mouse and Me!

1

Student Book

OXFORD
UNIVERSITY PRESS

Written by **Alicia Vázquez** and **Jennifer Dobson**

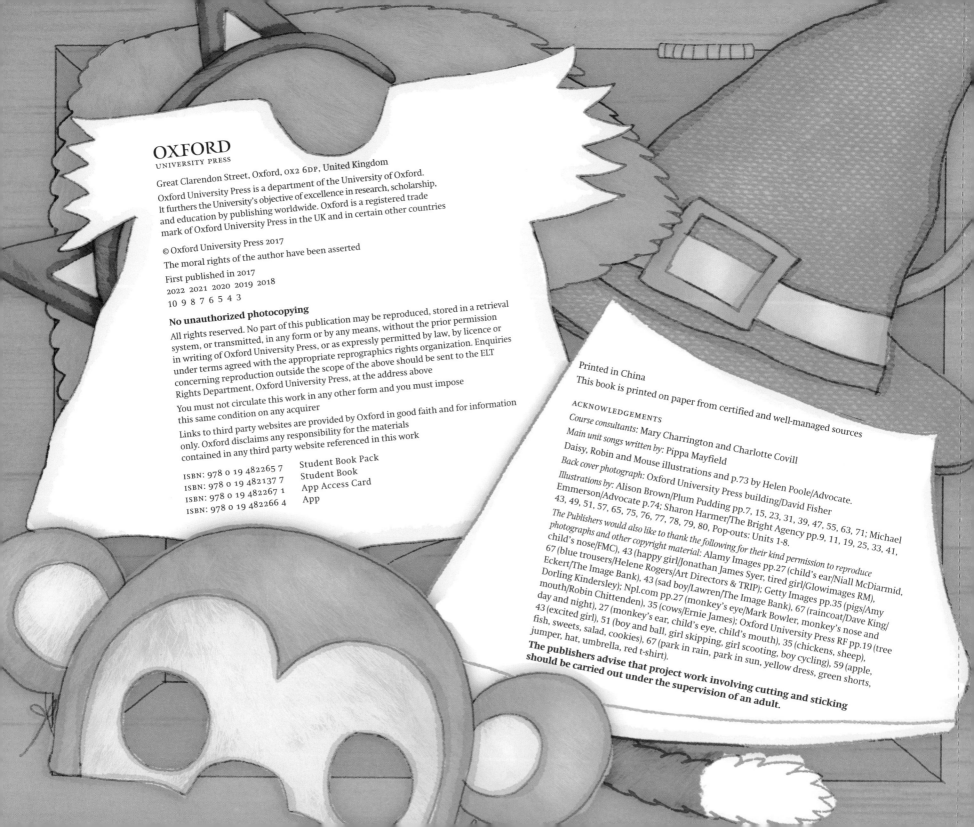

OXFORD
UNIVERSITY PRESS

Great Clarendon Street, Oxford, OX2 6DP, United Kingdom

Oxford University Press is a department of the University of Oxford.
It furthers the University's objective of excellence in research, scholarship,
and education by publishing worldwide. Oxford is a registered trade
mark of Oxford University Press in the UK and in certain other countries

© Oxford University Press 2017

The moral rights of the author have been asserted

First published in 2017

2022 2021 2020 2019 2018
10 9 8 7 6 5 4 3

ISBN: 978 0 19 482265 7   Student Book Pack
ISBN: 978 0 19 482137 7   Student Book
ISBN: 978 0 19 482267 1   App Access Card
ISBN: 978 0 19 482266 4   App

Printed in China

This book is printed on paper from certified and well-managed sources

ACKNOWLEDGEMENTS

Course consultants: Mary Charrington and Charlotte Covill

Main unit songs written by: Pippa Mayfield

Daisy, Robin and Mouse illustrations and p.73 by Helen Poole/Advocate.

Back cover photograph: Oxford University Press building/David Fisher

Illustrations by: Alison Brown/Plum Pudding pp.7, 15, 23, 31, 39, 47, 55, 63, 71; Michael
Emmerson/Advocate p.74; Sharon Harmer/The Bright Agency pp.9, 11, 19, 25, 33, 41,
43, 49, 51, 57, 65, 75, 76, 77, 78, 79, 80, Pop-outs: Units 1-8.

The Publishers would also like to thank the following for their kind permission to reproduce
photographs and other copyright material: Alamy Images pp.27 (child's ear/Niall McDiarmid,
child's nose/FMC), 43 (happy girl/Jonathan James Syer, tired girl/Glowimages RM),
67 (blue trousers/Helene Rogers/Art Directors & TRIP); Getty Images pp.35 (pigs/Amy
Eckert/The Image Bank), 43 (sad boy/Lawren/The Image Bank), 67 (raincoat/Dave King/
Dorling Kindersley); Npl.com pp.27 (monkey's eye/Mark Bowler, monkey's nose and
mouth/Robin Chittenden), 35 (cows/Ernie James); Oxford University Press RF pp.19 (tree
day and night), 27 (monkey's ear, child's eye, child's mouth), 35 (chickens, sheep),
43 (excited girl), 51 (boy and ball, girl skipping, girl scooting, boy cycling), 59 (apple,
fish, sweets, salad, cookies), 67 (park in rain, park in sun, yellow dress, green shorts,
jumper, hat, umbrella, red t-shirt).

**The publishers advise that project work involving cutting and sticking
should be carried out under the supervision of an adult.**

Hello!

Hello!

Daisy's new words

red   blue

- Point to Daisy, Robin and Mouse. Colour Robin's shorts and Daisy's skirt .
- Draw yourself.

Red and blue song

Red, red, red, red and blue,
Blue, blue, blue, blue and red,
Red, red, red, red and blue,
Blue, blue, blue, blue and red.

Point to something red,
Point to something blue,
Point to something red!

Point to something blue,
Point to something red,
Point to something blue!

(Repeat song)

- Sing the Red and blue song.

1   2   3

Hello!

Robin's new words

1	2	3

- Point and count: 1, 2, 3.
- Match. Colour Mouse .

Numbers song

1, 2, 3; 1, 2, 3,
Come on, count,
Count with me.
1, 2, 3; 1, 2, 3,
Come on, count,
Count with me.

1, 2, 3; 1, 2, 3,
Come on, count,
Count with me.
1, 2, 3; 1, 2, 3,
Come on, count,
Count with me.

Come on, count,
Count with me.

- Sing the Numbers song.

Hello!

At nursery school

books

- Find 3 books. Circle.

Unit 1 I want to be a wizard

Robin's new words

red   blue   yellow   green

- Find and stick.

Colours song

Stir, stir the magic pot.
Bubble, bubble, bubble.

Red, red in the pot!
Abracadabra!

Stir, stir the magic pot.
Bubble, bubble, bubble.

Blue, blue in the pot!
Abracadabra!

Stir, stir the magic pot.
Bubble, bubble, bubble.

Yellow, yellow in the pot!
Abracadabra!

Stir, stir the magic pot.
Bubble, bubble, bubble.

Green, green in the pot!
Abracadabra!

Red, blue, yellow, green.
Bubble, bubble, bubble!

Red, blue, yellow, green.
Abracadabra!

- Sing the Colours song.

Unit 1

Nature smart

rainy   sunny   rainbow

- Look and draw a rainbow.
- Point and say.

Rainbow song

It's rainy. It's rainy. Can you see a rainbow?
Pitter, patter. Pitter, patter. No, no, no!

It's sunny. It's sunny. Can you see a rainbow?
Shine, shine, shine, shine. No, no, no!

It's rainy. It's sunny. I can see a rainbow!
Pitter, patter. Shine, shine. Yes, yes, yes!

- Sing the Rainbow song.

Unit 1

Portfolio

Show what you can do

- Draw the paths to the rainbow from ⬤, ⬤, ⬤ and ⬤. Point to and say the colours.

- Circle your favourite colour.

- Where's Mouse? Find and point.

Notes

Unit

At nursery school

bag   crayon   book

- Look around your classroom. Point to a bag, a book and a crayon. Colour.
- Draw your school bag.

School song

What can you see?
A bag. A bag.
Look, a bag. Look, a bag.
What can you see?
A bag. A bag.
At my school.

What can you see?
A crayon. A crayon.
Look, a crayon. Look, a crayon.
What can you see?
A crayon. A crayon.
At my school.

What can you see?
A book. A book.
Look, a book. Look, a book.
What can you see?
A book. A book.
At my school.

- Sing the School song.

Unit 2 I want to be a hedgehog

Daisy's new words

| mummy | daddy | brother | sister |

- Find and stick.

Family song

Here's my mummy! Here's my daddy!
Here they are! Here they are!
Look! Here's my brother!
Look! Here's my sister!
Here they are! Here they are!

I love Mummy! I love Daddy!
Yes, I do. Yes, I do.
And I love my brother.
And I love my sister.
Yes, I do. Yes, I do.

(Repeat song)

- Sing the Family song.

Unit

Nature smart

day   night

- Look and colour: day ⬤ and night ⬤.

Day and night song

Some animals sleep in the day.
Some animals sleep in the day.
Some animals sleep in the day.
But children play all day.

Some animals play at night.
Some animals play at night.
Some animals play at night.
But children sleep all night.

- Sing the Day and night song.

10

Unit 2

Portfolio

Show what you can do

- Draw yourself and your family.
- Point and say.
- Where's Mouse? Find and point.

Notes

Unit

At nursery school

| granny   grandad |

- Point to Granny and Grandad. Follow the paths to school.
- Draw yourself and the person who takes you to school. Follow the path.

Granny and Grandad song

Who takes you to school?
Who takes you to school?
Granny. Granny.
She takes me to school.

Who takes you to school?
Who takes you to school?
Grandad. Grandad.
He takes me to school.

Who takes you to school?
Who takes you to school?
Mummy. Mummy.
She takes me to school.

Who takes you to school?
Who takes you to school?
Daddy. Daddy.
He takes me to school.

- Sing the Granny and Grandad song.

Unit 3 I want to be a monkey

Robin's new words

head   body   arms   legs

- Find and stick.
- Complete the legs and the arms.

Body song

(Chorus) I'm a monkey. I'm a monkey.
Ooh, ooh, ooh, ooh, oooh.

Nod, nod, nod your head.
Nod your head with me.
1, 2, 3, 4. Nod your head with me.

(Chorus)

Turn, turn, turn your body.
Turn your body with me.
1, 2, 3, 4. Turn your body with me.

(Chorus)

Wave, wave, wave your arms.
Wave your arms with me.
1, 2, 3, 4. Wave your arms with me.

(Chorus)

Kick, kick, kick your legs.
Kick your legs with me.
1, 2, 3, 4. Kick your legs with me.

I'm a monkey. I'm a monkey.
Ooh, ooh, ooh, ooh, oooh.

- Sing the Body song.

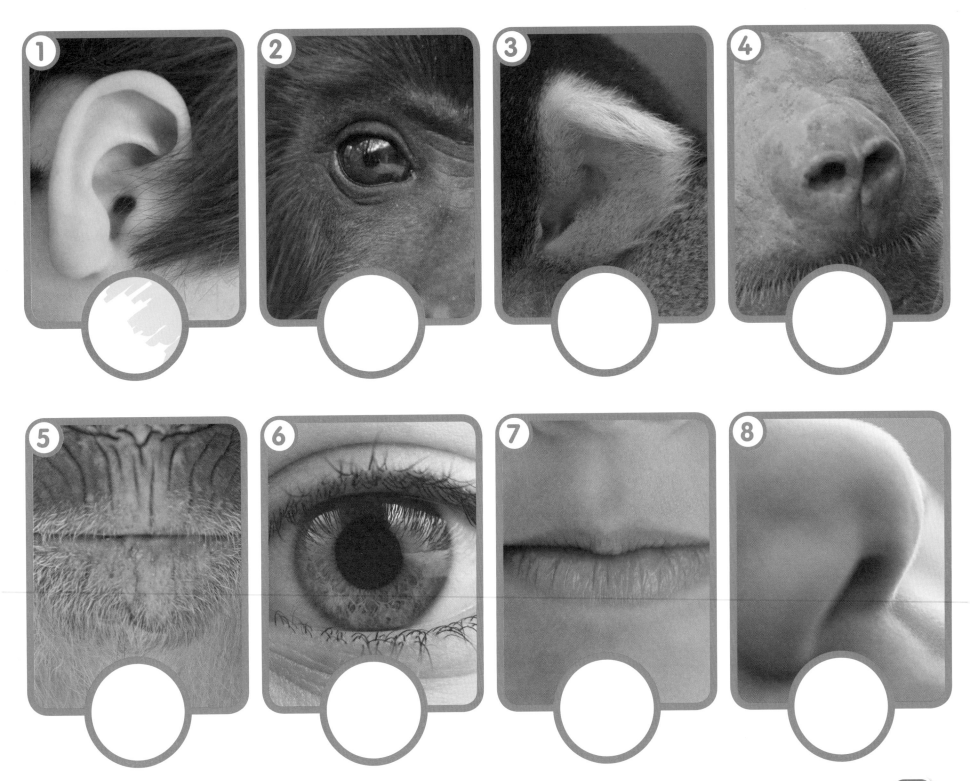

Body smart

nose   mouth   eyes   ears

- Look, match and colour: nose , mouth ,
  ear and eye .

- Point and say.

Face song

One, one. I've got one nose.
One, one. I've got one nose.
One, one. I've got one nose.
And a very happy mouth.

One, two. I've got two ears.
One, two. I've got two ears.
One, two. I've got two ears.
And a very happy mouth.

One, two. I've got two eyes.
One, two. I've got two eyes.
One, two. I've got two eyes.
And a very happy mouth.

- Sing the Face song.

14

Unit 3

Portfolio

Show what you can do

- Point and say.
- Draw yourself in the jungle.
- Where's Mouse? Find and point.

Notes

 1 ②3

 1 2 3

 1 2 3

Unit

At nursery school

| Stand up!   Sit down!   Walk! |

- Look and count. Circle the numbers.
- Stand up, sit down and walk!

Actions song

Let's all stand up!
Stand up! Stand up!
Let's all sit down!
Sit down! Sit down!
Let's all stand up!
Stand up! Stand up!
And walk around.
And walk around.

Let's all sit down, down, down.
Let's all stand up, up, up.
And walk around.
Oh, yes, oh, yes!
Let's all sit down, down, down.
Let's all stand up, up, up.
And walk around.
Oh, yes, oh, yes!

- Sing the Actions song.

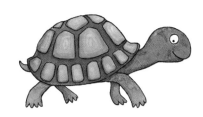

Unit 4 I want to be a cat

Daisy's new words

tortoise   dog   rabbit   fish

- Find and stick.
- Circle the tortoises ◯, the dogs ◯, the rabbits ◯ and the fish ◯.

Animals song

Look! I'm a tortoise!
Munch, munch, munch.
Look! I'm a tortoise!
Munch, munch, munch.
Look! I'm a tortoise!
Munch, munch, munch.
Munch, munch, munch, like this.

Look! I'm a dog.
Woof, woof, woof.
Look! I'm a dog.
Woof, woof, woof.
Look! I'm a dog.
Woof, woof, woof.
Woof, woof, woof, like this.

Look! I'm a rabbit.
Boing, boing, boing.
Look! I'm a rabbit.
Boing, boing, boing.
Look! I'm a rabbit.
Boing, boing, boing.
Boing, boing, boing, like this.

Look! I'm a fish.
Splash, splash, splash.
Look! I'm a fish.
Splash, splash, splash.
Look! I'm a fish.
Splash, splash, splash.
Splash, splash, splash, like this.

- Sing the Animals song.

1 ② 3

1 2 3

1 2 3

1 2 3

Unit

Nature smart

sheep   pig   cow   chicken

- Look and count. Circle the numbers.
- Point and say.

Farm animals song

'Baa, baa!' says the sheep.
'Baa, baa!' says the sheep.
Here on the farm, here on the farm.
Listen to the animals here on the farm.

'Oink, oink!' says the pig.
'Oink, oink!' says the pig.
Here on the farm, here on the farm.
Listen to the animals here on the farm.

'Moo, moo!' says the cow.
'Moo, moo!' says the cow.
Here on the farm, here on the farm.
Listen to the animals here on the farm.

'Cluck, cluck!' says the chicken.
'Cluck, cluck!' says the chicken.
Here on the farm, here on the farm.
Listen to the animals here on the farm.

- Sing the Farm animals song.

18

Unit 4

Portfolio

Show what you can do

- Point and say.
- Draw yourself on the farm.
- Where's Mouse? Find and point.

Notes

Unit

At nursery school

hamster   bird   kitten

- Match the children and the pets.
- Point and say.

Pets song

What's your favourite pet?
What's your favourite pet?
A hamster, a hamster.
Crunch, crunch, crunch!

What's your favourite pet?
What's your favourite pet?
A bird, a bird.
Cheep, cheep, cheep!

What's your favourite pet?
What's your favourite pet?
A kitten, a kitten.
Meow, meow, meow!

- Sing the Pets song.

Unit 5 I want to be a train driver

Robin's new words

| postman | doctor | teacher | cleaner |

- Find and stick.

Jobs song

What's your job?
What's your job?
I'm a postman.
Working every day.
I'm a postman.
Working every day.

What's your job?
What's your job?
I'm a doctor.
Working every day.
I'm a doctor.
Working every day.

What's your job?
What's your job?
I'm a teacher.
Working every day.
I'm a teacher.
Working every day.

What's your job?
What's your job?
I'm a cleaner.
Working every day.
I'm a cleaner.
Working every day.

- Sing the Jobs song.

Self smart

tired   excited   sad   happy

- Match the photos and the balloons.
- Colour the balloons: ●, ●, ● and ●.
- Point and say.

 Feelings song

How are you? How are you?
How are you today?
I'm tired, I'm tired,
I'm tired today.

How are you? How are you?
How are you today?
I'm excited, I'm excited,
I'm excited today.

How are you? How are you?
How are you today?
I'm sad, I'm sad,
I'm sad today.

How are you? How are you?
How are you today?
I'm happy, I'm happy,
I'm happy today.

- Sing the Feelings song.

Unit 5

Portfolio

Show what you can do

- Point and say.
- Draw yourself on the train. How do you feel? Circle.
- Where's Mouse? Find and point.

Notes

Unit

At nursery school

> dinner lady   secretary

- Colour the dinner lady and secretary.
- Draw your teacher.

School people song

A dinner lady works at school,
Busy, busy at our school.
We see her every day at school,
We wave and say hello. HELLO!

A secretary works at school,
Busy, busy at our school.
We see her every day at school,
We wave and say hello. HELLO!

A teacher works at school,
Busy, busy at our school.
We see her every day at school,
We wave and say hello. HELLO!

- Sing the School people song.

Unit **6** I want to be a shopkeeper

Daisy's new words

| teddy | car | doll | dinosaur |

- Find and stick.

Toys song

I've got a teddy. Yes, I have.
I've got a teddy. Yes, I have.
I've got a teddy. Yes, I have.
Cuddly teddy. Aaaaah!

I've got a car. Yes, I have.
I've got a car. Yes, I have.
I've got a car. Yes, I have.
Brrm, brrm, brrm.

I've got a doll. Yes, I have.
I've got a doll. Yes, I have.
I've got a doll. Yes, I have.
Rock, rock, rock-a-bye.

I've got a dinosaur. Yes, I have.
I've got a dinosaur. Yes, I have.
I've got a dinosaur. Yes, I have.
Roar, roar, roar.

- Sing the Toys song.

Body smart

bike   ball   scooter   skipping rope

- Look, match and colour: bike ⬤, ball ⬤, scooter ⬤ and skipping rope ⬤.
- Circle the actions you can do.

Outdoor toys song

Boys and girls, come out to play.
Bring a bike! Come and play!
Ride, ride, all day long.
Bring a bike! Come and play!

Boys and girls, come out to play.
Bring a ball! Come and play!
Bounce, bounce, all day long.
Bring a ball! Come and play!

Boys and girls, come out to play.
Bring a scooter! Come and play!
Zoom, zoom, all day long.
Bring a scooter! Come and play!

Boys and girls, come out to play.
Bring a skipping rope! Come and play!
Skip, skip, all day long.
Bring a skipping rope! Come and play!

- Sing the Outdoor toys song.

Unit 6

Portfolio

Show what you can do

- Point and say.
- Draw yourself in the playground.
- Where's Mouse? Find and point.

Notes

1 2 ③ 4

1 2 3 4

1 2 3 4

Unit

At nursery school

truck   jigsaw   robot

- Look and count. Circle the numbers.

- Draw your favourite toy.

Favourite toys song

What's your favourite toy?
It's my truck. It's my truck.
I like playing with my truck.
It's my favourite toy.

What's your favourite toy?
It's my jigsaw. It's my jigsaw.
I like playing with my jigsaw.
It's my favourite toy.

What's your favourite toy?
It's my robot. It's my robot.
I like playing with my robot.
It's my favourite toy.

- Sing the Favourite toys song.

Unit 7 I want to be a baker

Robin's new words

bread   milk   apple   eggs

- Find and stick.
- Match.

Food song

I need bread, I need bread for a sandwich.
I need bread for a sandwich, oh, yes!
I need bread, I need bread for a sandwich.
Be careful! Don't make a mess!

I need milk, I need milk for a milkshake.
I need milk for a milkshake, oh, yes!
I need milk, I need milk for a milkshake.
Be careful! Don't make a mess!

In the kitchen! In the kitchen!
I like cooking. Yes, I do. (Repeat)

I need apples, I need apples for a pie.
I need apples for a pie, oh, yes!
I need apples, I need apples for a pie.
Be careful! Don't make a mess!

I need eggs, I need eggs for a cake.
I need eggs for a cake, oh, yes!
I need eggs, I need eggs for a cake.
Be careful! Don't make a mess!

In the kitchen! In the kitchen!
I like cooking. Yes, I do. (Repeat)

- Sing the Food song.

Unit

Body smart

fish   sweets   salad   biscuits

- Look and circle the healthy food ⃝.
- Point and say.

Healthy food song

Fish is healthy! Let's have lots of fish.
Fish is healthy! Let's have lots of fish.
Fish, fish! Let's have lots of fish.
Yes, it's healthy food.

Sweets are yummy! Not too many, please.
Sweets are yummy! Not too many, please.
Sweets, sweets! Not too many, please.
They aren't healthy food.

Fish and salad,
Sweets and biscuits,
Fish, salad, sweets and biscuits.
La, la, la, la, la.

Salad is healthy! Let's have lots of salad.
Salad is healthy! Let's have lots of salad.
Salad, salad! Let's have lots of salad.
Yes, it's healthy food.

Biscuits are yummy! Not too many, please.
Biscuits are yummy! Not too many, please.
Biscuits, biscuits! Not too many, please.
They aren't healthy food.

Fish and salad,
Sweets and biscuits,
Fish, salad, sweets and biscuits.
La, la, la, la, la.

- Sing the Healthy food song.

Unit 7

Portfolio

Show what you can do

- Draw your favourite food.
- Point and say.
- Where's Mouse? Find and point.

Notes

Unit

At nursery school

| hot lunch   cold lunch |

- Colour the hot lunch 🟤 and the cold lunch 🔵.
- Draw your lunch.

Lunch song

Are you having hot lunch?
Are you having hot lunch?
Are you having hot lunch
At school today?

Are you having cold lunch?
Are you having cold lunch?
Are you having cold lunch
At school today?

Yes, I'm having fish.
Yes, I'm having fish.
Yes, I'm having fish
For lunch today.

Yes, I'm having sandwiches.
Yes, I'm having sandwiches.
Yes, I'm having sandwiches
For lunch today.

- Sing the Lunch song.

Unit 8 I want to be a pirate

Daisy's new words

dress   shorts   hat   T-shirt

- Find and stick.

Clothes song 1

Dressing up! Dressing up!
What can you see in the dressing-up box?
Look, a dress. Look, a dress.
Look, a dress. Put it on!

Dressing up! Dressing up!
What can you see in the dressing-up box?
Look, some shorts. Look, some shorts.
Look, some shorts. Put them on!

Dressing up! Dressing up!
What can you see in the dressing-up box?
Look, a hat. Look, a hat.
Look, a hat. Put it on!

Dressing up! Dressing up!
What can you see in the dressing-up box?
Look, a T-shirt. Look, a T-shirt.
Look, a T-shirt. Put it on!

- Sing Clothes song 1.

32

Self smart

trousers   jumper   jacket   umbrella

- Match the clothes and the weather.

Clothes song 2

Pitter patter rain. Pitter patter rain.
Wear your trousers. Look!
Look! It's rainy weather.

Pitter patter rain. Pitter patter rain.
Wear your trousers and your jumper. Look!
Look! It's rainy weather.

Pitter patter rain. Pitter patter rain.
Wear your trousers and your jumper
and your jacket. Look!
Look! It's rainy weather.

Pitter patter rain. Pitter patter rain.
Take your umbrella, wear your trousers
and your jumper and your jacket. Look!
Look! It's rainy weather.

- Sing Clothes song 2.

Unit 8

Portfolio

Show what you can do

- Draw yourself on holiday with Daisy and Robin.
- Point and say.
- Where's Mouse? Find and point.

Notes

Unit

At nursery school

| suitcase | sunglasses | swimsuit |

- Complete the pictures.
- Draw something to take on holiday.

Holiday song

What are you taking?
What are you taking?
What are you taking on your holiday?

I've got my suitcase.
I've got my suitcase.
I've got my suitcase. For my holiday.

What are you taking?
What are you taking?
What are you taking on your holiday?

I've got my swimsuit.
I've got my swimsuit.
I've got my swimsuit. For my holiday.

What are you taking?
What are you taking?
What are you taking on your holiday?

Oh, my sunglasses!
Oh, my sunglasses!
Oh, my sunglasses! For my holiday!

- Sing the Holiday song.

Birthdays

Birthdays

Happy Birthday!

> balloon   card   cake   party

- Point and say.
- Find, count and colour.
- Say *Happy Birthday!*

Happy Birthday song

Happy, happy Birthday,
Happy, happy Birthday!
I can see a card and I can see
a cake.

Happy, happy Birthday,
Happy, happy Birthday!
I can see a balloon!
Oh, four balloons!

Happy Birthday!
Come and see the cake,
Come and see the card,
Join the party!

(Repeat song)

- Sing the Happy Birthday song.

Christmas

Christmas

Happy Christmas!

> Father Christmas   present   Christmas tree

- Colour 1 ●, 2 ● and 3 ●.

Christmas song

Father Christmas is coming,
Let's go to sleep.
He will leave some presents
By your Christmas tree.
Hurry, hurry, hurry!
It's getting late.
Father Christmas is coming,
Time to go to bed.
Goodnight, goodnight.
Happy Christmas, everyone!

(Repeat song)

- Sing the Christmas song.

Easter

Easter

Happy Easter!

> basket   flower   egg

- Help the rabbit find the eggs.
  Draw and colour the eggs.

Easter song

Hello, hello, hello Mr Rabbit,
Come on, come on, come on find your eggs.
Put them, put them, put them in your basket,
Play, play, play the Easter game!

Hello, hello, hello Mr Rabbit,
Come on, come on, come on find your eggs.
Put them, put them, put them in your basket,
Play, play, play the Easter game!

Among the flowers, look!
Among the flowers, look!
Among the flowers,
You can see the eggs.

Among the flowers, look!
Among the flowers, look!
Among the flowers,
You can see the eggs.

- Sing the Easter song.

Summer

1 (2) 3

1 2 3

1 2 3

39

Summer

Happy holidays!

> beach   towel   bucket

- Count and circle. Colour.

 Summer song

(Chorus) Summer, summer, summer,
Summer at the beach,
With Mummy and Daddy,
And all my family!

Summer, summer, summer,
Summer at the beach,
With Mummy and Daddy,
And all my family!

Playing with my bucket, playing in the sand,
Can I have my bucket, my bucket please?

(Chorus)

Now I need my towel to go for a swim.
Can I have my towel, my towel please?

(Chorus)

- Sing the Summer song.

Unit 6 Body smart Outdoor toys

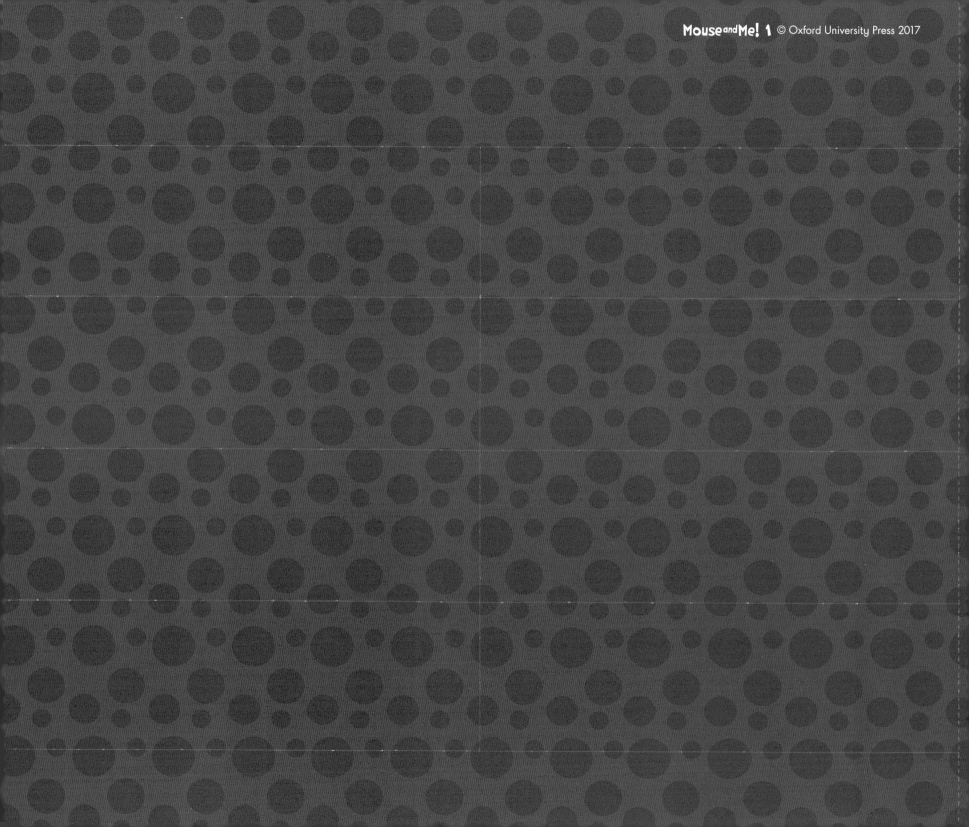

Unit 5 Self smart Feelings

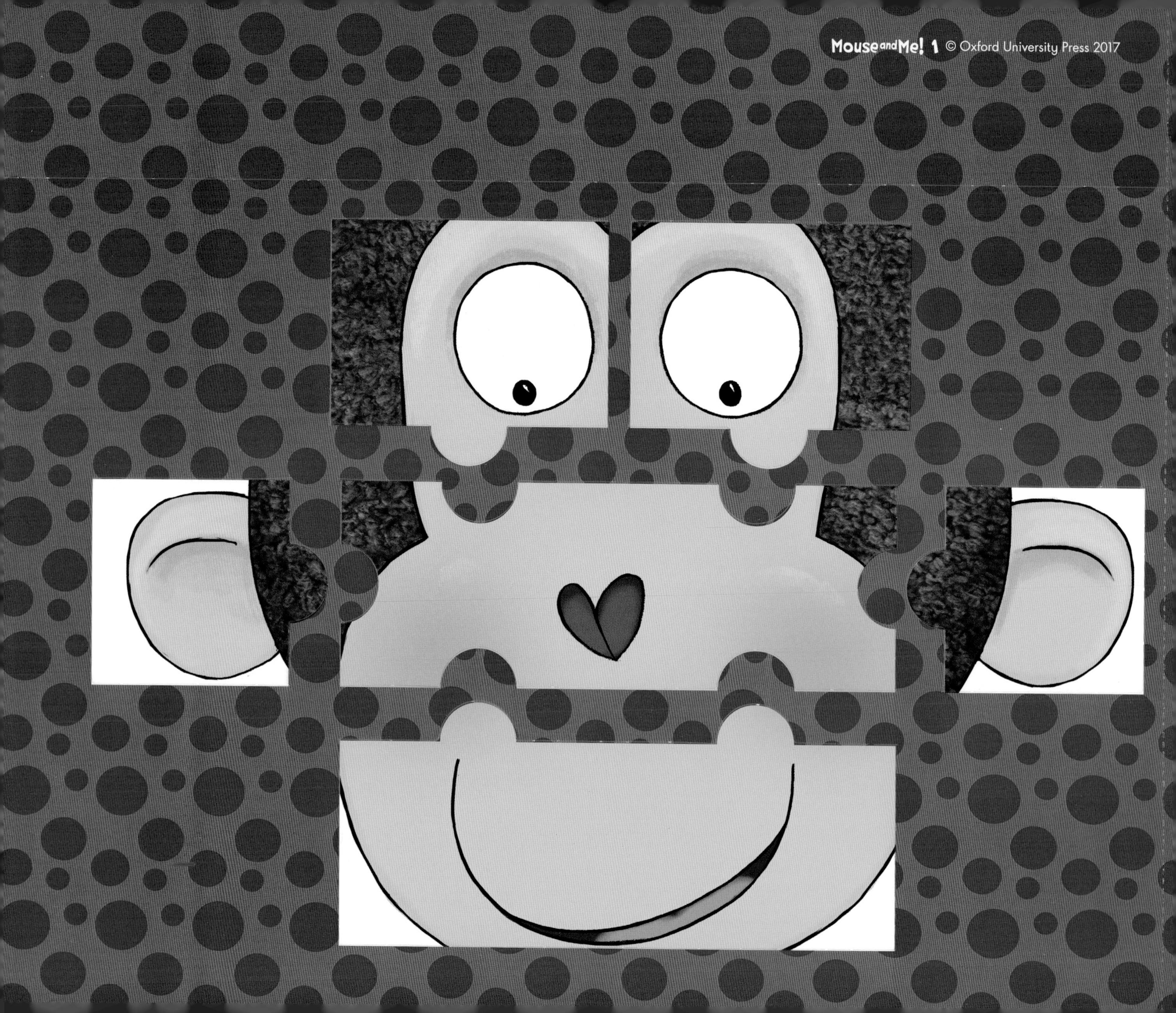

Unit 7

Unit 7

Unit 7

Unit 7

Unit 8

Unit 8

Unit 8

Unit 8

Costume stickers